Contents

Why Convene a Forum on Campus Sex Crimes?

On January 25, 2012, the U.S. Department of Justice's Office for Victims of Crime (OVC), Office on Violence Against Women (OVW), and Office of Community Oriented Policing Services (COPS) partnered with the International Association of Campus Law Enforcement Administrators and the U.S. Department of Education's Office for Civil Rights (OCR) to conduct a forum to discuss ways to enhance criminal investigations of campus sex crimes. OVC convened the forum at the urging of leaders in the campus law enforcement field who saw a critical need to support campus public safety agencies in determining how best to facilitate effective sex crimes investigations. However, there was little formal consensus among the leaders regarding what constitutes promising practices specific to sex crimes investigations in higher education settings.

The forum comprised representatives from college law enforcement, student affairs, campus sexual assault victim services, government agencies, national organizations that focus on campus safety or address public policy issues for higher education more broadly, and organizations or individuals that provide legal counsel or risk management tools for colleges and universities. Forum participants were asked to identify the following:

- Challenges, issues, and promising practices related to investigating campus sex crimes.
- Resources that exemplify promising practices or that may be useful in their implementation.
- Key partners in campus sex crimes investigations and potential coordination challenges.
- Suggestions to help guide criminal investigations of campus sex crimes.

This report summarizes the key outcomes from this forum; the views and opinions reflected in this report do not necessarily reflect the views of the participating federal agencies.

Several factors underscored the need to convene the forum, held in Washington, D.C.:

- **High rates of sexual assault, coupled with low rates of reporting to law enforcement.** It is estimated that nearly 20 percent of women and 6 percent of men will be victims of sexual assault during their college years (Krebs et al., 2007). Yet, just as in the community at large, sex crimes that occur on college and university campuses are vastly underreported to the criminal justice system. For example, one study suggests that as few as 12 percent of college rape victims report their assault to the police (Kilpatrick et al., 2007).

- **Public safety agencies differ among colleges, universities, and other institutions of higher education, and each plays a unique role in sex crimes investigations.** For example, some institutions have campus police agencies that investigate sex crimes, while others have campus security operations that refer reports of sex crimes to local law enforcement. Because these differences can affect sex crimes investigations—in addition to the differences in state laws and local resources regarding sexual assault—a single prescribed approach to sex crimes investigations will not work for every campus. However, forum participants agreed on the need for practical guidance that would begin with summarizing the similarities and differences among campus public safety agencies.

- **Most campus sexual assaults are committed by an acquaintance of the victim rather than by a stranger**. Acquaintance sexual assault is among the most difficult of crimes to prove because oftentimes little evidence is available to show that nonconsensual sexual contact occurred. Campus police agencies sometimes lack the specialized training needed to investigate these complex cases. Additionally, successful criminal adjudication hinges on campus public safety agencies coordinating their efforts with the local criminal justice system, and this coordination is not easily accomplished or sustained.

- **Local law enforcement agencies may have to coordinate their investigation of a campus sex crime with the school's investigation**. Certain sex crimes may be reported to the college or university and constitute a violation of the school's student code of conduct or Title IX of the Education Amendment of 1972 (Title IX), 20 U.S.C. §1681 et seq., which prohibits discrimination on the basis of sex in educational settings that receive federal financial assistance. On April 4, 2011, OCR issued a Dear Colleague Letter to clarify how Title IX applies to sexual violence on campus and remind schools of their Title IX responsibilities (Dear Colleague Letter). The letter reiterates that if a school knows, or reasonably should know, about student-on-student harassment that creates a hostile environment, Title IX requires the school to take "immediate action" to eliminate the harassment, prevent its recurrence, and address its effects. After the letter was issued, questions were raised regarding the mechanics of parallel criminal and Title IX investigations, which may occur due to a school's Title IX obligation to take "immediate action" to address the alleged harassment.

The forum's 1-day meeting was sufficient to generate considerable information and ideas but it was not enough time to explore concerns in depth or to come to consensus about the essential national-level guidance that campus public safety agencies need to enhance their sex crimes investigations. With this in mind, this report includes the forum's recommendations for continuing this dialogue and building consensus.

Key Terms

This report focuses on campus sex crimes rather than school-based sexual misconduct violations or Title IX sexual harassment violations. Any mention of campus sexual misconduct or sexual harassment primarily relates to concerns regarding parallel investigations conducted by a school pursuant to its Title IX obligation to address alleged sexual harassment and by local or campus law enforcement as part of a criminal investigation, or the need to educate campus communities about the spectrum of behaviors these violations cover, their distinguishing features, and the remedies, options, and resources proposed for each type of violation. For the purposes of this report, key terms are defined as follows:

- *Sex crimes* refers to a narrowly defined group of sexual acts that are considered criminal by a specific local, state, federal, or tribal jurisdiction. The governing jurisdiction in which the college or university is located codifies which acts are considered sex crimes. Examples of specific crimes include rape, sexual assault, and sexual battery.
- *Sexual violence* is used in the Dear Colleague Letter to refer to "physical sexual acts perpetrated against a person's will or where a person is incapable of giving consent due to the victim's use of drugs or alcohol." The letter also specifies that an individual may be unable to give consent due to an intellectual or other disability. Victim advocacy organizations often use sexual violence as an umbrella term to describe a wider spectrum of behaviors, but for the purposes of this report, sexual violence is limited to those acts covered by the Dear Colleague Letter.

- ***Campus sexual misconduct*** refers to forms of sexual behavior that a college or university identifies as a violation of its institutional policies (e.g., student codes of conduct). This includes sex crimes as well as other sexual behaviors that are not criminal in nature.
- ***Sexual harassment***, under Title IX, refers to unwelcome conduct of a sexual nature, including unwelcome sexual advances, requests for sexual favors, and other verbal, nonverbal, or physical conduct of a sexual nature. Harassment creates a hostile environment if the conduct is sufficiently serious that it interferes with a student's ability to participate in or benefit from the school's programs. Sexual violence is a form of sexual harassment prohibited by Title IX.

Suggestions From the Forum

The suggestions offered by forum participants were preliminary and included some overlapping themes. Continued dialogue is recommended to assess the usefulness and viability of these suggestions for the campus public safety field to enhance its capacity to investigate sex crimes. For detailed explanations of these suggestions, see the Suggestions for Practice Guidance section on page 8.

1. **Build campus public safety capacity for investigating sex crimes.**
   - Customize each campus public safety agency's response to sex crimes for its specific role within the institution, while maintaining compliance with all relevant laws.
   - Sustain a customized approach by institutionalizing policies and practices within the campus public safety agency and its institution, in conjunction with relevant local agencies.
   - Assess the students' comfort level regarding reporting incidents and seeking services.
   - Encourage further dialogue to clarify what campus public safety agencies should do with information about a sex offense if a victim discloses an incident but does not want to officially report the crime, be identified, or be involved in a criminal investigation.

2. **Strengthen the institutional response to campus sex crimes.**
   - Educate upper-level campus administrators on the complexities of responding to campus sex crimes. Urge them to support effective campus-wide action to respond to and prevent sex crimes.
   - Promote education on sex crimes for students, faculty, and staff.
   - Encourage campus public safety agencies to actively support school-based sex crime prevention efforts.

3. **Enhance coordination among campus public safety officers, other campus responders, and local responders.**
   - Recognize the essential roles that coordination and communication among campus and local responders play in effective criminal investigations of campus sex crimes.

- Encourage dialogue on coordination and communication issues among institutional leaders, campus public safety agencies, victim advocates, and local law enforcement representatives and prosecutors who regularly work with colleges and universities.
- Seek guidance from OCR on the mechanics of conducting parallel investigations, including how the "immediate action" requirements affect criminal investigation procedures.
- Promote the development of memorandums of understanding (MOUs) with relevant entities to clarify roles and coordination responsibilities. MOUs should be signed by agency leaders who have the power to make or change their agency's policies.
- Support the use of formal structures to facilitate a coordinated team approach among campus and community partners to responding to campus sex crimes (e.g., sexual assault response teams (SART) and policy or resource teams).
- Provide the multidisciplinary training necessary to promote coordination and communication among responders.

4. **Increase training opportunities for campus public safety officers.**
    - Train campus public safety officers in how to respond to sex crimes.
    - Encourage each institution to have at least one officer in its campus public safety department with specialized training and experience on responding to sex crimes.

Suggestions for Practice Guidance

The forum provided an initial opportunity to discuss what practice guidance the campus public safety field could benefit from to enhance its capacity to investigate sex crimes. The preliminary suggestions offered during the forum comprised several overlapping themes that address four main objectives:

1. Build campus public safety capacity for investigating sex crimes.
2. Strengthen the institutional response to campus sex crimes.
3. Enhance coordination among campus public safety officers, other campus responders, and local responders.
4. Increase training opportunities for campus public safety officers.

These suggestions are explained in detail below. Continued dialogue is recommended to more thoroughly explore and expand on these suggestions and to assess their usefulness and feasibility. See the Resources section for information on the resources mentioned during the forum, as well as additional resources the campus public safety field may find helpful.

1. **Build campus public safety capacity for investigating sex crimes.**
   A. **A campus public safety agency's response to campus sex crimes should be customized for the agency's specific role within the institution, while maintaining compliance with relevant laws**. A "one size fits all" approach won't work—colleges and universities are distinct in myriad ways, as are campus public safety agencies and local law enforcement agencies (see *Challenge: Differences Shape Approaches*, page 10). That said, there are established and emerging promising practices related to responding to sex crimes that campus public safety agencies should consider. Each agency is encouraged to customize its approach to its agency-specific roles and jurisdictional definitions of sex crimes, adjust to institutional needs to the extent possible (without compromising investigations), creatively maximize its resources, promote institutional policies and local collaborations that support effective response, and be flexible enough in its approach that it can address challenges as they arise. A college or university's customized approach, however, must still comply with relevant laws such as Title IX.

To implement a customized response, campus public safety agencies should have policies and procedures in place to guide specifically how officers handle sex crime reports. The policies and procedures should take into consideration factors such as threat assessments, the Sexual Assault Victims' Bill of Rights, and the requirements of the Jeanne Clery Disclosure of Campus Security Policy and Campus Crime Statistics Act (Clery Act).[i] Agency guidelines should also explain how to address these factors in different types of cases and circumstances, not just broadly.

Forum participants suggested the following tools for promoting a consistent response:

- Officer training on discipline-specific procedures and forms, as well as on coordination procedures within the institution and with community partners.
- Templates for officer communication with victims and offenders.
- Checklists for officers to follow during their initial response to the incident (e.g., palm cards).
- Written materials for victims on what to do if they are a victim of crime, the types of assistance available, and the criminal justice process.
- A review of sexual assault reports by a supervisor or chief to ensure proper steps were taken in each case.

Campus public safety procedures for responding to sex crimes should be publicized to ensure that students know what to expect if they seek assistance and how to locate related services (e.g., through links to those services on the public safety department's Web page). Campus public safety agencies should periodically update their contact lists of on- and off-campus resources. In addition, agency procedures should clearly differentiate between the initial response processes for campus police and security departments (as security departments lack police powers), describe the differences between the agency's response to recent reports versus delayed reports, and facilitate the involvement of a victim advocate as early as possible in interactions with victims.[ii] It may also be useful for campus public safety agencies to explore investigative practices effectively used in other crime areas and whether they might apply in cases of sex crimes.

Challenge: Differences Shape Approaches

A "one size fits all" approach to developing campus public safety agency responses is impractical because colleges and universities differ in myriad ways, as do campus public safety departments and local law enforcement agencies. Educational institutions can vary in location, size, type of school (public or private, degrees or certifications offered, religious affiliation, etc.), student demographics, majors offered, academic rigor, faculty and student affairs staffing, campus environment and facilities, housing options, social activities, Greek life, and athletic programs.

The types of campus public safety agencies include campus police departments staffed by officers who have full police powers, that function as part of a college or university; security departments staffed by security personnel who do not have full police powers, that function as part of a college or university and rely on municipal, county, or state police for support in criminal matters; private firms contracted by a college or university to provide security services; and municipal, county, or state police agencies that provide police services to a college or university by contract or agreement. Some campus police and security operations are also responsible for patrolling areas that surround campuses through agreements with local or state law enforcement authorities or legislation. On large campuses, police and security services may be provided by more than one agency (Mid-Atlantic Regional Community Policing Institute, 2004).

Establishing oversight authority for a campus public safety agency may pose additional problems. The designation of which local law enforcement agency or agencies have jurisdiction over a college or university or the surrounding area also varies (e.g., there may be one law enforcement agency or several law enforcement agencies that serve the area and could potentially be involved).

B. **Sustaining a customized approach requires the institutionalization of uniform policies and practices within the campus public safety agency and its institution, in conjunction with relevant local agencies.** Institutionalizing policies and practices can also help build trust between campus public safety agencies and the campus community at-large.

C. **Campus public safety agencies should assess the students' comfort level in reporting to them and seeking their services.** Effective criminal response to campus sex crimes is all but impossible if students are not reporting these offenses (see *Challenge: Underreporting*, page 13). Campus public safety agencies should assess why victims of sex crimes may or may not seek their assistance and consider what changes are needed to remove any barriers identified. If victims are undecided about reporting, agencies should think of new ways to encourage victims to seek help, report victimization, and facilitate the preservation of evidence. For example, offering alternatives to traditional reporting methods—such as instituting anonymous reporting procedures, third-party reporting procedures, and accepting initial reports by e-mail or texting—may increase students' comfort level enough that they will report their assault.

Campus public safety agencies should consider ways to enhance their relationships with students, so that students are comfortable reporting to them when a crime occurs. After all, some students only encounter public safety officers when there is a problem (e.g., underage drinking situations) and may have a less-than-positive impression of campus officers. However, when public safety officers get involved in student activities (e.g., by speaking at prevention programs or being present at school events), students are more likely to develop positive perceptions of them.

Campus public safety agencies also should engage as allies others to whom victims might disclose sex crimes, such as faculty, staff, student paraprofessionals and leaders, or local service providers. It is important for campus public safety agencies to engage these potential allies and educate them about options for reporting, assistance available to students, and how to respond to student disclosures, as appropriate for their roles. Engaging these different groups will likely require different strategies and partnerships.

D. **Encourage further dialogue to clarify what campus public safety agencies should do with information about a sex offense if the victim discloses an incident but does not want to officially report a crime, be identified as a victim to others, or be involved in**

a criminal investigation. Campus public safety agencies have different approaches to sex crimes cases in which victims do not want to report or participate in investigations. In some instances, a victim's decision to not be involved will close the criminal case. However, some institutions require their campus public safety agencies to share information about sexual victimization or the potential threat posed by a sex offender with campus officials (e.g., a dean of students or Title IX coordinator). Some campus public safety agencies also may share information about the incident with local law enforcement to check for patterns of crime (e.g., a serial rapist).

A discussion of best practices in these situations should involve, at a minimum, campus public safety officials, victim advocates, institutional leaders, and local law enforcement. The discussion should address the following questions:

- What is the campus public safety agency's responsibility to the victim in these situations? When, if ever, does community protection override victim confidentiality?
- How does the campus public safety agency determine exceptions to victim confidentiality beyond state mandatory reporting requirements? What Clery Act and Title IX obligations (and any other legal mandates) apply to campus public safety agencies?
- How does the campus public safety agency store information provided by a victim who does not want to officially report or by a third party, in case the victim wants to participate in an investigation at a later time or the agency wants to establish crime patterns if they receive additional similar reports?

It is important to clarify questions related to victim confidentiality so that campus public safety officers can accurately explain to students the scope and limits of confidential communications if they disclose sexual victimization. Campus public safety officers should also be able to inform students about the scope of confidentiality that other responders can offer them in these cases.

Challenge: Underreporting

The majority of victims of sex crimes do not report their victimization to law enforcement, and those who do may delay reporting. There are many reasons student victims may not report, or may delay reporting, sex crimes. For example—

- They do not identify what they experienced as sexual assault.
- They do not see themselves as crime victims with a right to report.
- They believe the assault was their fault.
- They have heard their peers (e.g., on social media outlets) blaming other victims of sexual assaults and are afraid they will blame them too and/or side with the perpetrator.
- They do not want to get the perpetrator in trouble.
- They interpret the incident as a one-time misunderstanding, not realizing that perpetrators often target individuals they view as vulnerable and susceptible to their manipulation (e.g., individuals who are drunk, have a disability, etc.).
- They do not want to disappoint their parents.
- They do not feel comfortable going to campus public safety officers (e.g., because they don't view them as particularly friendly or don't know what to expect in terms of a response).
- They are hesitant to take legal action or be involved in justice system proceedings.
- They are afraid of getting in trouble if they were drinking or using drugs illegally when the assault occurred.

2. **Strengthen institutional response to sex crimes.**
   A. **Educate upper-level administrators at colleges and universities on the complexities involved in responding to campus sex crimes, and urge their commitment to support effective campus-wide response and prevention efforts.** This top-down endorsement should translate into a strong institutional plan for responding to and preventing sex crimes that is posted and widely distributed to the campus community. Campus public safety agencies can request that specific practices be incorporated into the plan, such as—
      - Victims' immediate access to a sexual assault victim advocate who can provide support, information, and assistance to victims (whether they report or not) and

partner with campus public safety agencies and other responders to aid victims. Some schools have in-house sexual assault victim advocates, while others rely on community-based advocacy services.

- Victims' access to staff trained through sexual assault forensic examiner programs, where available, who can provide medical forensic examinations.
- Timely coordination among all responders to a disclosure of a sex crime.[iii]

Forum participants also recommended that campus public safety agencies assess how institutional and student cultures affect perceptions and the likelihood of campus sex crimes, as well as reactions to it. Results could be used to facilitate dialogue with upper-level administration on the need for an enhanced campus-wide response to sex crimes.

B. **Promote education for students, faculty, and staff on sex crimes.** Students are the primary audience for education on sex crimes. However, faculty, staff, and student paraprofessionals and leaders may be approached by students who have experienced or witnessed sex crimes and therefore should be trained to know what to say to these students and to make referrals.[iv] Campus public safety agencies can stress to the institution the need for education on the following topics:

- The spectrum of nonconsensual sex acts that are considered sex crimes in the jurisdiction, differentiated from school sexual misconduct violations and Title IX violations (also identifying where overlaps exist).
- How the college or university responds to and works to prevent sex crimes.
- The general meaning of "nonconsensual" in sexual situations (e.g., students cannot give consent to a sexual act if their ability to consent is compromised by alcohol or drugs, and silence is not permission).
- What victims can do if they experience a sex crime.
- The range of assistance available to victims on- and off-campus, such as services, information, and social media tools that encourage or help victims access assistance.
- Victims' options in terms of criminal, school disciplinary, and civil remedies, and the scope of privacy they can anticipate with each remedy.

- Whether or not prosecutors or the school typically grants immunity or amnesty to student victims who may have been voluntarily drinking underage or using illegal drugs in the course of a sex crime.
- The impact of delayed reporting or non-reporting of sex crimes.
- The importance of bystander intervention in preventing sex crimes.

Campus public safety agencies can support colleges and universities in pursuing increasingly creative ways to deliver these educational messages to students. Traditionally, colleges have presented this information during new student orientation. There is good reason for this timing—students are at an increased risk of sexual victimization during their first weeks of school (sometimes referred to by campus violence prevention educators as the "red zone"). In addition, there is a greater risk of sexual victimization for first-year students and sophomores than for juniors and seniors (Gross et al., 2006). However, students are typically overloaded with information during orientation, and some students, particularly commuters, elect not to participate in orientation activities. Forum participants offered the following suggestions for alternative or additional approaches to educating students on this topic:

- Utilize online learning venues and social media to communicate with students.
- Use a combination of school staff, local partners (e.g., rape crisis centers), and peer or student advocates and leaders to educate the campus community.
- Offer programs and information over the summer preceding a student's first year.
- Provide programs and information for parents.
- Supplement in-person presentations with video sessions.
- Visit students where they live (e.g., have resident assistants do related activities with students in their residences, have other student leaders reach out to commuter students at off-campus locations.)
- Change presentation tactics (e.g., talk to students as friends, rather than potential victims, who can help if one of their peers experiences a sex crime.)

- Involve the institution's marketing department, encourage sororities and fraternities to compete for the best tagline on marketing pieces, and distribute marketing products (wristbands, buttons, bumper stickers, etc.) that reinforce the message.
- Supplement prevention programming on alcohol-facilitated sexual assault with other tactics (e.g., by having peer advocates hang sheets from trees with the message "alcohol is not consent" written on them.)
- Tie participating in sex crime educational activities into matriculation (e.g., require students to complete an online course on sex crimes in order to graduate, require that students make at least three related campus contacts such as with a police officer, victim advocate, or counselor prior to registering for classes.)

C. **Campus public safety agencies should take an active role in supporting school-based sex crimes education and prevention efforts.** Involvement in these programs can signal to students that the agency wants to be an ally in preventing sex crimes and to help students when sex crimes occur. Also, having at least one officer with whom students feel comfortable as a point-of-contact might encourage and influence students to seek out campus public safety assistance if a sex crime occurs.

Encourage colleges and universities to support an approach to sex crimes prevention that includes efforts both to reduce the risk of victimization and to prevent perpetration. Risk reduction strategies—what students can do to reduce their risk of experiencing sex crimes—play an important role in campus prevention efforts (e.g., disseminating tips on reducing risk in social situations, educating students on healthy relationships, sponsoring rape aggression defense programs). Ideally, these strategies should be paired with primary prevention activities aimed at stopping perpetration. One important primary prevention tool is bystander intervention programming that mobilizes bystanders to intervene when they see acts of violence or situations that are likely to escalate to violence. By intervening, bystanders can help redirect peer pressure toward healthy and respectful social norms (Tabachnick, 2009).

3. **Enhance coordination among campus public safety, other campus responders, and local responders.**

   A. **Recognize the essential roles that coordination and communication among responders—both on campus and locally—play in effective criminal investigations of campus sex crimes.** Campus public safety agencies and others involved in responding to sex crimes on campus must know each other's roles. Understanding each other's roles helps lessen tensions that may exist among responders and increases opportunities to jointly assist students and move forward with criminal investigations. In addition, building relationships among responders is critical to coordinating criminal investigations with concurrent school sexual misconduct or Title IX investigations and in being able to promptly and comprehensively address problems that arise in cases.

   B. **Encourage dialogue on coordination and communication issues in campus sex crime cases among institutional leaders; campus public safety agencies; local law enforcement representatives and prosecutors who regularly work with colleges and universities; and victim advocates.** Possible questions to address include the following:[v]

   - Are there ways that campus public safety agencies or the schools themselves can engage their local prosecution offices and build support for criminal investigations of campus sex crimes? Support is needed particularly in "word against word" cases (she said/he said situations in which there is little obvious evidence to prove lack of consent to the sexual contact.) Campus public safety agencies may question the utility of proceeding with a criminal investigation if there is a pattern of "word against word" sex crime cases being declined by prosecutors. Although law enforcement may take criminal action upon the showing of probable cause in a case, prosecutors often exercise discretion in choosing the cases they prosecute.

   - How should campus police departments deal with the perception of some prosecutors and local law enforcement that campus police work for colleges and universities and therefore cannot be trusted to conduct impartial investigations? The perception may also be that to be impartial, these cases should be turned over to local law enforcement from a concurrent jurisdiction.

   - In what situations, if any, does local law enforcement take the lead in cases involving students from the college or university? What if the campus public safety agency is a police department? What if it is a security department? Who has jurisdiction for incidents involving students that were committed off campus? Are there any agreements in place between agencies that indicate jurisdiction for both agencies and procedures for making referrals? Are there differences in their coordinated response when there is a delayed report of an incident versus a timely report of a recent incident?

- How should campus public safety agencies obtain feedback from local law enforcement and prosecutors regarding investigation outcomes for cases involving college or university students? Obtaining feedback can be difficult; even when there is a good relationship between agency leaders, the same relationship may not exist between staff of different agencies (e.g., a campus criminal investigator and a local investigator in a specialized unit or an assistant prosecutor). Establishing a feedback loop with key individuals in the local criminal justice system is critical to the agency's ability to address problems that arise in cases and strengthen investigative outcomes over time.

- To what extent is information sharing across agencies appropriate in a particular case? For example, what information can a campus police department share with a college or university related to a criminal investigation? What information can local law enforcement agencies that are handling an off-campus case involving students share with the college or university if they are conducting a Title IX or school sexual misconduct investigation? If a case is not officially reported to the campus public safety agency or a victim does not want to be involved in a case, can campus public safety agencies check in with local law enforcement regarding, for example, whether similar patterns of perpetration were seen in other cases? What are the logistics of information sharing in each of these cases?

- How can electronically stored evidence (including from social media outlets) be useful in campus sex crimes investigations? College students make abundant use of electronic devices to communicate. Electronically stored communication between victims, offenders, witnesses, friends, and others related to a sex crimes case could have corroborative value in an investigation. What types of officer training and campus public safety procedures might be helpful to local law enforcement and prosecutors in terms of electronic communications?

- Does the college or university have an agreement with local child protection services for instances of suspected child sexual abuse and procedures for coordinating a response with local governmental entities, such as child protective services?

C. **Seek guidance from OCR on the mechanics of conducting parallel investigations as indicated in its Dear Colleague Letter.** Also, seek OCR's input regarding concerns about how a school's obligation to take "immediate action" to address sexual harassment may impact criminal investigation procedures. During the forum, campus police agencies and local law enforcement agencies voiced concerns regarding how this requirement could potentially affect their ability to conduct criminal investigations. In general, forum participants requested clarity on how to coordinate parallel criminal and Title IX investigations. OCR's Dear Colleague Letter states that schools should not wait for the conclusion of a criminal investigation or criminal proceeding to begin their own Title IX investigation and, if needed, must take immediate steps to protect the student in the educational setting.[vi] For example, a school should not delay conducting its own investigation or taking steps to protect the complainant because it wants to see whether the alleged perpetrator will be found guilty of a crime. Any agreement or memorandum of understanding (MOU) with a local police department must allow the school to meet its Title IX obligation to resolve complaints promptly and equitably.[vii] Although a school may need to delay temporarily the fact-finding portion of a Title IX investigation while police gather evidence, once notified that the police department has completed its gathering of evidence (not the ultimate outcome of the investigation or the filing of any charges), the school must promptly resume and complete its fact-finding for the Title IX investigation (Dear Colleague Letter, 10).

Several questions and issues related to Title IX and the coordination of investigations were raised during the forum. For example—[viii]

- What are the logistics of information sharing in specific cases? Is sharing information appropriate among investigators and without victim permission? When is communication with and consent of a victim vital? For example, what if a case

19

involving two students from different schools is being criminally investigated by campus police at the institution where the crime occurred, as well as investigated as a student code of conduct violation at another institution? What steps should be taken if there is a Title IX investigation and investigators believe there is enough evidence for a criminal investigation? What if, in the process of an administrative investigation, investigators learn of new physical evidence? Are there protocols for if, when, and how investigators should share that new evidence with others, either within the same institution or at other institutions? These questions illustrate the potential complexity of multiple investigations and the need for coordination, as different investigations may have different pieces of relevant information.[ix]

- How should we best encourage dialogue among OCR, campus public safety agencies, school administrators, victim advocates, and local law enforcement and prosecution on how to handle a school's Title IX obligations in individual cases? OCR representatives at the forum suggested contacting regional OCR offices for advice.

- If local law enforcement has charged an individual in a campus sex crime case and a trial is pending, law enforcement investigators might be reluctant to testify in a parallel school disciplinary hearing. Although law enforcement reports can be obtained by affidavit, pertinent information is often located in investigative notes rather than the report. Local law enforcement agencies may be concerned about defense attorneys using testimony from the school's disciplinary hearing as a means of discovery in the criminal case.

D. **Develop MOUs with relevant entities to clarify roles and coordinate responsibilities.** MOUs should be signed by agency leaders who have the power to make or change agency policies. MOUs, and subsequent multidisciplinary training to implement MOUs, can lay the groundwork for building and sustaining relationships among the institution, campus public safety agency, and local law enforcement and prosecution.

E. **Promote the use of formal structures to facilitate a coordinated team approach among campus and community partners for responding to campus sex crimes, such as sexual assault response teams (SARTs) and policy or resource teams.** Criminal investigations can be negatively impacted by a lack of coordination and communication among responders and decisionmakers. A team approach can help overcome such problems, and will be more effective if it is supported by upper level administration with, for example, MOUs to help formalize the process of facilitating coordination.

Encourage the creation of a campus-based SART or participation in an existing local SART to improve the initial response to campus sex crimes. SARTs are multidisciplinary teams that provide a specialized immediate response to sexual assault. Such a team can facilitate coordinated, immediate interventions and services, including victim support, medical care, evidence collection and documentation, and the initial criminal investigation (Office on Violence Against Women, 2004). A SART can help victims make informed decisions about their participation in each step of the initial response process by educating them about their options, the possible consequences associated with those options, and the resources available to them. Ultimately, a SART can help ensure that campus and local responders work together to aid victims and hold offenders accountable. Like community-based SARTs, campus SARTs should be customized to the specific needs of the campus and its student population.

A campus-based SART should comprise representatives from campus public safety, local law enforcement (if campus public safety is provided by a security department), and victim advocacy (on- or off-campus), and include a sexual assault medical forensic examiner (typically a sexual assault nurse examiner). It is helpful if prosecutors are available or on-call to consult with responders as needed. Other school and community agencies and professionals may be involved, depending on the resources available from the institution and the community, as well as the specifics of a case (e.g., residence life staff may be involved if there are immediate concerns related to campus housing.)

Note that team members do not have to come together physically to provide interventions, but they should follow protocols that allow them to coordinate their responses to the extent possible. They can also meet periodically to discuss ways to improve the team's overall performance. As an alternative to or in addition to a campus SART, campus representatives can also participate in a local SART, if one exists. In some instances, cases on college campuses may generate considerable activity for a local SART.

Schools should also consider forming a campus policy or resource team, with members meeting periodically to make decisions about institutional policies related to sex crimes, support SART efforts, and address other related coordination concerns. Stakeholders can include, but are not limited to, campus public safety agencies; victim advocacy groups; health services representatives; student affairs representatives (residence life, dean of students, etc.); prevention education programs; campus clergy; campus entities addressing the needs of lesbian, gay, bisexual, transgendered, and questioning (LGBTQ) student populations; student counseling services; the Title IX coordinator; and the institution's general counsel and insurer (the scope and limitations of the roles of these last two stakeholders on the team should be further explored). Campus policy and resource teams also can encourage the participation of policymakers from involved community agencies, including representatives from local law enforcement, prosecution, hospitals, forensic examiner programs, and victim service programs such as rape crisis centers.

Promote dialogue among campus public safety agencies, campus SARTs, policy teams, and other campuses that have representatives on local SARTs to learn more about the logistics of implementing and sustaining a SART-like structure and a policy or resource team, and the specific roles of law enforcement. SARTs and policy teams are not quick fixes—collaboration takes time, resources, and effort to overcome barriers to development and sustainability. However, a team approach to the initial response to sex crimes in the community has been shown to be effective in facilitating timely response, victim assistance, and collection of forensic evidence and initial information gathering by law enforcement.

Also, given the complex overlay of institutional policies and governmental requirements in these cases, it is critical to have an oversight team to coordinate an institution's response to sex crimes with the criminal justice response to these crimes. Even for nontraditional and small campuses, assembling responders and taking steps to improve response is a worthwhile task. The main concern for these campuses is how to develop such entities with little resources and support.

F. **Multidisciplinary training is necessary for promoting coordination and communication among responders.** Training helps ensure that all partners are on the same page regarding the response to sex crimes specific to the campus setting, applicable criminal laws, the mechanics of complying with legal mandates, implementation of protocols and policies, and coordination of criminal investigations with parallel school investigations, among other issues. Also, training various constituencies together helps build relationships across offices and agencies. More discussion is needed to identify related training topics, develop curricula, and determine what guidance can be offered for implementing such training in different institutional settings.

4. **Increase Training Opportunities for Campus Public Safety Officers**

A. **Campus public safety officers should be trained on responding to sex crimes, as specific to their agency role.** Sex crimes are some of the most difficult types of crimes to prove, particularly in "word against word" cases where the issue is not whether the sexual contact occurred, but whether it occurred without consent. In these cases, there is often little physical evidence and few witnesses to corroborate lack of consent. Because of this, conducting these types of investigations is even more challenging when the crime is reported days, weeks, or months after the fact.

Despite the complexity and seriousness of these cases, campus public safety officers typically receive more training on other areas of public safety (e.g., traffic investigations). Training on sex crimes is critical for campus officers who initially respond to or investigate campus sex crime reports, and for those who lead their agencies. Both campus police and security departments need guidance on how to conduct their initial response to reports of sex crimes. Campus police agencies also need guidance on criminal investigation strategies in college and university settings. Although security departments do not need training on criminal investigation strategies, they do need to know how to act as a liaison between the local criminal justice system and the institution related to these cases.

Several key training topics were mentioned during the meeting (some of which were identified as challenges or gaps in these cases and then translated into training topics.)

Training topics for all officers involved in campus sex crime response:

- Campus public safety agencies' roles and procedures in the initial response to a victim of a sex crime (noting that although there may be any number of agency points of contact for victims, officer response should be consistent and based on established agency policies and procedures.)

- Dynamics of perpetration (e.g., training on perpetrator grooming behaviors so officers understand that, rather than being random incidents, many sexual assaults are premeditated).

- Dynamics of sexual victimization, victim trauma, and behavior (e.g., to help officers understand victim actions, avoid making victim-blaming statements, and avoid inaccurately labeling a report as false).

- Potential short- and long-term victim needs in the aftermath of a sexual assault, and how a victim advocate can assist victims in identifying and addressing these needs.

- Coordination issues that often arise between campus and community partners in responding to campus sex crimes and the appropriate roles of these partners.

- Impact of relevant federal mandates on campus sex crimes cases and coordination issues.

- Options available to students related to criminal, school, and civil remedies; reporting; and victim assistance.

- Reasons for delayed reporting or failure to report sex crimes.

- The role of victim trauma, fear, and shame.

- Documentation or report writing.

- Prevention strategies that campus public safety agencies can support (e.g., bystander behavior and prevention).

<u>Training topics for criminal investigators</u>:

- Investigation strategies in sex crimes cases, both general and those that specifically address the campus setting.
- Specific guidance on "word against word" cases (e.g., training on shifting the investigative focus from victims to alleged offenders, proving lack of consent, the effect of alcohol on cases, and creatively gathering evidence and witness statements to provide more details about the nature of a reported incident).
- Investigative strategies for alcohol- or drug-facilitated sexual assaults.
- Interview techniques for obtaining case information while building trust between officer and victim.
- Accessing, using, and preserving electronically stored evidence.
- Specific coordination issues during the investigation.

Training could also be implemented for those in management or leadership positions, encompassing many of the topics listed above as well as issues such as customizing and institutionalizing policies and procedures, case review, coordination, SARTs, supporting education and prevention activities, etc.

To create a comprehensive training curriculum, further consideration should be given to refining and expanding on the topics listed above. Use of program tracks to provide role-specific training for first-responding officers, criminal investigators, management and leadership, etc., was also mentioned during the forum. To model the coordination needed in these cases, trainers should represent not only campus public safety agencies but also campus and community partners involved in responding to sex crimes (community law enforcement, prosecution, medical and forensic examiners, victim advocacy, etc.), as appropriate to the topic.

The logistics of training school officers across the country was preliminarily discussed during the forum and requires further dialogue. A national training program for campus public safety officers on sex crimes was suggested as a potentially efficient way to reach officers at all relevant levels and provide consistent information and opportunities for building skills. Underlying the dialogue about a potential national-level training effort was the acknowledgment that each campus public safety agency needs to customize its approach to its specific roles within its institution, but that there is much in the way of guidance for general practice that could be offered to campus public safety officers to support their agency's customized response.

Two of the training challenges identified were providing access to baseline training for campus police officers from institutions that lack resources or motivation to fund training, and accommodating officer work schedules despite the institution's need for public safety officer coverage. More conversation would be useful on the challenges posed to campus public safety agencies by training officers on how to respond to sex crimes.

B. **Each institution should have at least one officer in the campus police department with specialized training and experience in sex crimes investigation.** This may be in the form of a sex crimes unit or an officer identified as the sex crimes investigator. A campus police department might also partner with the local law enforcement agency to "shadow" a local law enforcement officer who specializes in investigating sex crimes. Similarly, a campus security department could have at least one officer with specialized training in how best to initially respond to sex crimes and to work with local law enforcement on these cases.

Next Steps

Forum participants offered the following recommendations for potential next steps in the effort to develop national-level practice guidance for criminal investigations of campus sex crimes:

1. Create a central online clearinghouse for sharing what campus public safety agencies and related national organizations are doing to promote effective criminal investigations of campus sex crimes. Possible functions for such a site include, but are not limited to, the following:

    - Showcasing success stories and encouraging replication of successes.[x]

    - Highlighting resources, promising practices, and grant-funded efforts.

    - Connecting campus public safety to resources.

    - Providing examples of low- or no-cost ways for campus public safety agencies to improve their investigation strategies in sex crimes cases.

    - Enabling dialogue among campus public safety personnel about related issues, problems, and solutions.

    - Polling campus public safety agencies on their policies, practices, and challenges related to sex crimes.

    - Identifying research needs and sharing the implications of related research.

    - Providing information about and links to trainings, technical assistance opportunities, and Web materials.

2. Use smaller working committees, ideally comprising participants from this forum and others, to continue this dialogue. Numerous suggestions were made for engaging in further discussion on particular topics. One was for small committees to discuss case scenarios specific to a topic, with the goal of further identifying gaps, issues, and promising practices. Small committees can also expand on preliminary forum suggestions for practice guidance, discuss implementation strategies, and further identify resources.

3. Expand efforts to help colleges and universities develop and sustain SARTs. Explore what training exists that colleges and universities could use to guide them in developing a campus SART or expanding a local SART to include school campuses. Even if an institution is not ready to create its own SART or get involved with an existing one, it may be useful to examine what principles of coordination and collaboration could be implemented without a

formal team structure. Campus public safety agencies should explore what technical assistance might be available or useful to assist them with such an examination.

4. Consider the benefits of using consortia that bring representatives from colleges and universities within a geographical area together to discuss shared issues, challenges, and possible solutions related to investigations of campus sex crimes. Consortia also provide an opportunity to reach out to other campuses in the vicinity to examine their practices.

5. Engage additional national organizations in the effort to enhance the effectiveness of criminal investigation of campus sex crimes. One suggestion provided is to "find stars who can push the issue." Further consideration and discussion are needed regarding which groups to engage and how best to engage them.

6. Further identify what training tools, training modules, and technical assistance on sex crimes investigations have been developed by national-level law enforcement organizations. Consider which tools can be adapted for college and university campus settings.

Endnotes

[i] See 20 U.S.C. § 1092(f).

[ii] The Title IX regulations require that schools publish notices of nondiscrimination stating that the institution does not discriminate on the basis of sex in its educational programs and activities. In the Dear Colleague Letter, OCR recommends that the nondiscrimination policy state that prohibited sex discrimination covers sexual harassment, including sexual violence, and that the policy includes examples of the types of conduct that it covers. OCR also recommends that the notice be prominently posted on school Web sites and at various locations throughout the campus and published in electronic and printed publications (Dear Colleague Letter, 6–7).

Among other things, the Clery Act requires institutions of higher education to publish and distribute an annual security report to all current students and employees, and make the report available upon request to prospective students and employees. The report must include, *inter alia*, statements of policy that address sex offenses and access to information on registered sex offenders in the campus community, including (1) a description of educational programs for promoting the awareness of rape, acquaintance rape, and other forcible and non-forcible sex offenses; (2) procedures students should follow if a sex offense occurs; (3) information on a student's option to notify appropriate law enforcement authorities; (4) notification to students of existing on- and off-campus counseling, mental health, or other student services for victims of sex offenses; (5) notification to students that the institution will change a victim's academic and living situations after an alleged sex offense, and the options for those changes if those changes are requested by the victim and are reasonably available; (6) procedures for campus disciplinary action in cases of an alleged sex offense; and (7) sanctions the institution may impose following a final determination of an institutional disciplinary proceeding regarding rape, acquaintance rape, or other forcible or non-forcible sex offenses. The institution must also include a statement advising the campus community where law enforcement agency information provided by a state concerning registered sex offenders may be obtained, such as the law enforcement office of the institution, a local law enforcement agency with jurisdiction for the campus, or a computer network address. In addition, institutions that have a campus police or security department must create, maintain, and make available a daily crime log; the institution must notify students and employees of the availability of the log, its contents, and its location. See U.S. Department of Education, Office of Postsecondary Education, *The Handbook for Campus Safety and Security Reporting,* Washington, D.C., 2011. This report is available on the Department's Web site at http://www.ed.gov/admins/lead/safety/campus.html.

[iii] Three additional practices were briefly mentioned in the discussion but without fully fleshed-out explanations. These ideas also are more under the authority of campus leadership than public safety. The first idea was to consider linking response to campus sex crimes to campus emergency management procedures to increase the attention these crimes received from upper level school administration. The second and third ideas pertained more to sexual misconduct violations than sex crimes. The second idea was that institutional explanations of sexual misconduct include consent-based definitions so that students understand the importance of giving and receiving consent to sexual activities. The third idea was that institutions consider it good practice to offer immunity (some call this amnesty) to victims for lesser violations they may have engaged in surrounding their victimization. Note that similar immunity/amnesty for victims in sex crimes cases depends on the jurisdiction's prosecution practices. The *National Protocol for Sexual Assault Medical Forensic Examinations* (2004) recommended "…before pursuing charges related to illegal drug or alcohol use by patients, prosecutors should give great weight to the impact that the threat of such charges may have on the patient's willingness to report the sexual assault and be involved in subsequent criminal justice proceedings." OCR's Dear Colleague Letter also includes a discussion of this issue. Schools should be aware that victims or third parties may be deterred from reporting incidents if alcohol, drugs, or other violations of school or campus rules were involved. As a result, schools should consider whether their disciplinary policies have a chilling effect on victims' or other students' reporting of sexual violence offenses. For example, OCR recommends that schools inform students that the school's primary concern is student safety, that any other rules

violations will be addressed separately from the sexual violence allegation, and that the use of alcohol or drugs never makes the victim at fault for sexual violence (Dear Colleague Letter, 15).

[iv] As discussed in OCR's Dear Colleague Letter, OCR recommends that all schools implement preventive education programs and make victim resources, including comprehensive victim services, available. Schools may want to include these education programs in their (1) orientation programs for new students, faculty, and staff; (2) training for students who serve as advisors in residence halls; and (3) training for student athletes and coaches. These programs should include a discussion of what constitutes sexual harassment and sexual violence, the school's policies and disciplinary procedures, and the consequences of violating these policies. The education programs should also include information aimed at encouraging students to report incidents of sexual violence to the appropriate school and law enforcement authorities. OCR also recommends that schools develop specific sexual violence materials that include the schools' policies, rules, and resources for students, faculty, coaches, and administrators. Schools should also include such information in their employee handbook and any handbooks that student athletes and members of student activity groups receive. These materials should include where and to whom students should go if they are victims of sexual violence. These materials also should tell students and school employees what to do if they learn of an incident of sexual violence. Schools also should assess student activities regularly to ensure that the practices and behavior of students do not violate the institutions' policies against sexual harassment and sexual violence (Dear Colleague Letter, 14–15).

[v] Although not specific to sex crimes in which campus police or local law enforcement investigate, the issue was raised of how a college or university should best address sex crimes and school sexual misconduct or Title IX violations that occur in foreign countries in student study-abroad situations. There is a need for dialogue on effective practices in this area. A suggestion was to research potential resources through various venues, such as U.S. Department of Defense, Peace Corps, FBI, U.S. State Department, and law enforcement oriented programs such as the International Association of Chiefs of Police.

[vi] Schools must conduct their own Title IX investigation because, although police investigations may be useful for fact-gathering, the standards for criminal investigations are different. Police investigations or reports are not determinative of whether sexual harassment or violence violates Title IX. Conduct may constitute unlawful sexual harassment under Title IX even if the police do not have sufficient evidence of a criminal violation. A criminal investigation does not relieve the school of its duty under Title IX to resolve complaints promptly and equitably. A school should notify a complainant of the right to file a criminal complaint, and should not dissuade a victim from doing so either during or after the school's internal Title IX investigation (Dear Colleague Letter, 10).

[vii] Nothing in an MOU or the criminal investigation should prevent a school from notifying complainants of their Title IX rights and the school's grievance procedures, or from taking interim steps to ensure the safety and well-being of the complainant and the school community while the law enforcement agency's fact-gathering is in progress. OCR also recommends that a school's MOU include clear policies on when a school will refer a matter to local law enforcement (Dear Colleague Letter, 10).

[viii] A related issue was raised specific to school-based investigations. Generally, colleges and universities are precluded from using local or state law enforcement and crime lab resources to collect, preserve, and/or analyze forensic evidence in a school sexual misconduct or Title IX violation investigation when (1) there is not a criminal investigation or (2) the case is declined for prosecution (and evidence is likely not analyzed by the jurisdiction). In these instances, how far should a college or university go to collect, preserve, and analyze evidence on its own? How far *can* a college or university go to collect, preserve, and analyze such evidence? Does the school have access to appropriate resources for these purposes? If not, will the school need to hire private firms? Where will the school get funding to do so? These are fact-specific, logistical questions that were not specifically addressed in OCR's Dear Colleague Letter. Colleges and universities may need to provide additional guidance to assist their campus security agencies in conducting comprehensive school sexual misconduct or Title IX violation investigations in the absence of a criminal case.

ix In states with mandatory reporting laws, schools may be required to report certain incidents to local law enforcement or child protection agencies.

x One participant told a story about a sheriff's daughter who fought for her friend to have access to a sexual assault medical forensic examination—her efforts were successful in part because she was aware of state law requiring hospitals to offer sexual assault victims who present at a hospital emergency department an exam for free with no questions asked.

References

Gross, A, et al. 2006. "An Examination of Sexual Violence Against College Women." *Violence Against Women* 12(3): 288–300.

Kilpatrick, D, et al. 2007. *Drug Facilitated, Incapacitated, and Forcible Rape: A National Study.* Charleston, SC: National Crime Victims Research and Treatment Center, www.ncjrs.gov/pdffiles1/nij/grants/219181.pdf.

Krebs, C. et al. 2007. *The Campus Sexual Assault Study Final Report.* Washington, DC: U.S. Department of Justice, www.ncjrs.gov/pdffiles1/nij/grants/221153.pdf.

Mid-Atlantic Regional Community Policing Institute. 2004. *National Summit on Campus Public Safety—Strategies for Colleges and Universities in a Homeland Security Environment,* Washington, DC: U.S. Department of Justice, Office of Community Oriented Policing Services.

Office on Violence Against Women. 2004. *A National Protocol for Sexual Assault Medical Forensic Examinations (Adults/Adolescents),* Washington, DC: U.S. Department of Justice.

Office for Civil Rights. 2011. *Sexual Violence Dear Colleague Letter.* Washington, DC: U.S. Department of Education, www.ed.gov/ocr/letters/colleague-201104.pdf.

Tabachnick, J. 2009. *Engaging Bystanders in Sexual Violence Prevention.* Enola, PA: National Sexual Violence Resource Center, www.nsvrc.org.

Resources

This list is not exhaustive; rather it is meant to help build a more comprehensive clearinghouse of resources related to campus sex crimes investigations.

Agencies and Organizations

If not already engaged in efforts to improve the response to campus sex crimes, these entities were noted in the forum as potential allies.

American College Personnel Association

http://www2.myacpa.org/

American Council on Education (ACE)

www.acenet.edu/AM/Template.cfm?Section=Home

ACE is a member organization that represents presidents and chancellors of institutions of higher education. It provides leadership on higher education issues and influences public policy through advocacy, research, and program initiatives. ACE fosters partnerships within and outside the higher education community to help colleges and universities anticipate and address challenges.

Bureau of Justice Assistance (BJA)

U.S. Department of Justice, Office of Justice Programs

www.bja.gov/Default.aspx

BJA provides leadership and services in grant administration and criminal justice policy development to support local, state, and tribal justice strategies to achieve safer communities. It supports programs and initiatives in the areas of law enforcement, justice information sharing, counterterrorism, managing offenders, combating drug crime and abuse, adjudication, advancing tribal justice, crime prevention, protecting vulnerable populations, and capacity building. BJA also supports law enforcement training initiatives that address or may be adapted to address campus sex crimes investigations.

Bureau of Justice Statistics (BJS)

U.S. Department of Justice, Office of Justice Programs

http://bjs.ojp.usdoj.gov/

BJS collects, analyzes, publishes, and disseminates information on crime, criminal offenders, victims of crime, and the operation of justice systems at all levels of government. Go to http://bjs.ojp.usdoj.gov/index.cfm?ty=pbo to access BJS publications.

End Violence Against Women International (EVAWI)

http://www.evawintl.org/

EVAWI focuses on connecting professionals in the field and strengthening the community's response to violence against women. EVAWI holds training conferences each year, offers consultation on best practices, provides training curricula and resource materials, distributes key research, and coordinates media campaigns. EVAWI's Online Training Institute offers numerous courses that speak to conducting sexual assault investigations (see http://olti.evawintl.org/images/courses/Brochure/OLTI-eFile.pdf).

Higher Education Resource Center for Alcohol, Drug Abuse, and Violence Prevention

U.S. Department of Education

www.higheredcenter.org/

The Higher Education Center for Alcohol, Drug Abuse, and Violence Prevention assists institutions of higher education in developing, implementing, and evaluating policies and programs that will foster students' academic and social development and promote campus and community safety.

International Association of Chiefs of Police (IACP)

www.theiacp.org

IACP is a member organization of police executives that offers an extensive training program and publications that speak to issues affecting police departments. Many of its trainings (e.g., The National Law Enforcement First-Line Supervisor Training on Violence Against Women) and publications may be of interest to those involved in investigating campus sex crimes.

International Association of Campus Law Enforcement Administrators (IACLEA)

www.iaclea.org/

IACLEA is the leading voice for the campus public safety community. It advances public safety for educational institutions by providing educational resources, advocacy, and professional development services. In addition to more than 1,200 college and university institutional members, IACLEA has 2,000 individual memberships held by campus law enforcement staff, criminal justice faculty members, and municipal chiefs of police.

Men Can Stop Rape (MCSR)

www.mencanstoprape.org/

MCSR seeks to mobilize men to use their strength for creating cultures free from violence, especially men's violence against women. It provides agencies, schools and organizations with direct services for youth, public service messaging, and leadership training. In contrast to traditional efforts that address men as the problem, MCSR's work embraces men as allies with the will and character to make healthy choices and foster safe, equitable relationships.

National Association of Student Personnel Administrators (NASPA)

http://naspa.org/

NASPA is an association of member organizations for college student affairs personnel and administrators that disseminates information and offers training to its members. NASPA and its members may be useful allies in engaging student affairs staff to help students who are sexually assaulted access services and report crimes.

National Center for Injury Prevention and Control (NCIPC), Division of Violence Prevention

Centers for Disease Control and Prevention

www.cdc.gov/ViolencePrevention/index.html

In 1992, the Centers for Disease Control and Prevention established NCIPC as the lead federal organization responsible for violence prevention. The Division of Violence Prevention is one of three divisions within NCIPC. For a wealth of resources on sexual violence prevention issues, go to http://www.cdc.gov/ViolencePrevention/sexualviolence/index.html.

National Collegiate Athletic Association (NCAA)

http://www.ncaa.org/

The NCAA was founded to protect student athletes while emphasizing both athletics and academic excellence. It comprises three membership classifications—Divisions I, II, and III. Each division creates its own rules governing personnel, amateurism, recruiting, eligibility, benefits, financial aid, and playing and practice seasons, consistent with the overall NCAA governing principles.

National District Attorneys Association (NDAA)

http://www.ndaa.org/

NDAA is a professional association representing criminal prosecutors that serves as a nationwide, interdisciplinary resource center for training, research, technical assistance, and publications for the prosecutorial profession.

National Institute of Justice (NIJ)

U.S. Department of Justice, Office of Justice Programs

http://nij.gov/

NIJ is dedicated to improving knowledge and understanding of crime and justice issues through science. NIJ provides information and tools for reducing crime and promoting justice. Go to www.nij.gov/nij/topics/a-z-index.htm to access information and research materials on specific topics.

National Resource Center on Sexual Violence (NSVRC)

www.nsvrc.org/

NSVRC is a national information and resource hub that collects and disseminates a wide range of resources on sexual violence including statistics, research, position statements, statutes, training curricula, prevention initiatives, and program information. Links to resources on campus sexual violence are available at www.nsvrc.org/saam/campus-resource-list.

Office for Civil Rights (OCR)

U.S. Department of Education

http://www2.ed.gov/about/offices/list/ocr/index.html

OCR works to ensure equal access to education and to promote educational excellence throughout the Nation through vigorous enforcement of civil rights. OCR serves student populations facing discrimination as well as advocates and institutions promoting systemic solutions to civil rights problems. It also resolves complaints of discrimination. Agency-initiated cases, typically called *compliance reviews*, permit OCR to target resources on compliance problems that appear particularly acute. OCR also provides technical assistance to help institutions achieve voluntary compliance with the civil rights laws that OCR enforces. An important part of OCR's technical assistance is its partnerships designed to develop creative approaches to preventing and addressing discrimination. For technical assistance, contact the regional office for your state (see http://wdcrobcolp01.ed.gov/CFAPPS/OCR/contactus.cfm).

Office of Community Oriented Policing Services (COPS)

U.S. Department of Justice

www.cops.usdoj.gov/

COPS advances the practice of community policing in state, local, and tribal law enforcement agencies. It works principally by sharing information and making grants to police departments throughout the United States. COPS offers an extensive training program and publications that may be of interest to those investigating campus sex crimes.

Office of Law Enforcement Coordination (OLEC)

Federal Bureau of Investigation (FBI)

www.fbi.gov/about-us/office-of-law-enforcement-coordination

OLEC serves as the primary liaison between FBI Headquarters and national associations representing state, local, tribal, and campus law enforcement agencies. Specific to campus public safety, OLEC staff connect campus agencies to FBI and other federal agencies' resources.

Office of Postsecondary Education (OPE)

U.S. Department of Education

http://www2.ed.gov/about/offices/list/ope/index.html

OPE formulates federal postsecondary education policy and administers programs that address critical national needs in support of its mission to increase access to quality postsecondary education.

Office for Victims of Crime (OVC)

U.S. Department of Justice, Office of Justice Programs

www.ovc.gov/welcome.html

Established in 1988 through an amendment to the Victims of Crime Act (VOCA) of 1984, OVC is charged by Congress with administering the Crime Victims Fund (the Fund). Through OVC, the Fund supports a broad array of programs and services that focus on helping victims in the immediate aftermath of crime and continuing to support them as they rebuild their lives. Millions of dollars are invested annually for victim compensation and assistance in every U.S. state and territory, as well as for training, technical assistance, and other capacity-building programs designed to enhance service providers' ability to support victims of crime in communities throughout the Nation.

Office for Victims of Crime Training and Technical Assistance Center (OVC TTAC)

www.ovcttac.gov/

OVC TTAC provides training and technical assistance for victim service providers and allied professionals who serve crime victims. It draws on the expertise of a network of consultants and seasoned victim service professionals with experience in designing and delivering customized responses to satisfy a variety of training and technical assistance needs. OVC TTAC can provide developmental support, mentoring, and facilitation to assist with program design and implementation, strategic planning, program management, evaluation, quality improvement, collaboration, and community coordination.

Office on Violence Against Women (OVW)

U.S. Department of Justice

www.ovw.usdoj.gov/

OVW provides federal leadership in developing the Nation's capacity to reduce violence against women and administer justice for and strengthen services to victims of domestic violence, dating violence, sexual assault, and stalking. It administers financial and technical assistance to communities across the country that are developing programs, policies, and practices aimed at ending these crimes. OVW also administers three formula-based and 18 discretionary grant programs, established under VAWA and subsequent legislation.

OVW's Campus Grant Program (Grants to Reduce Domestic Violence, Dating Violence, Sexual Assault, and Stalking on Campus Program) encourages institutions of higher education to adopt comprehensive, coordinated responses to domestic violence, dating violence, sexual assault, and stalking. Through this grant program, campuses, in partnership with community-based nonprofit victim advocacy organizations and local criminal justice or civil legal agencies, adopt protocols and policies that treat violence against women as a serious offense and develop victim service programs that ensure victim safety, offender accountability, and the prevention of such crimes. Information about applying for these campus grants is available through the OVW Web site.

Police Executive Research Forum (PERF)

http://policeforum.org/

PERF is a police research organization and a provider of management services, technical assistance, and executive-level education to support law enforcement agencies. It helps to improve the delivery of police services through the exercise of national leadership, public debate of police and criminal justice issues, and research and policy development. One recent publication of interest to those involved in campus sex crimes investigations is *Improving Police Response to Sexual Assault*, a report on a 2011 PERF conference that brought together approximately 150 police executives, leaders of women's and crime victim organizations, FBI leaders and other federal officials, and others to explore weaknesses in the investigation of sexual assault crimes.

Rape, Abuse and Incest National Network (RAINN)

www.rainn.org/

RAINN created and operates the National Sexual Assault Hotline (800–656–HOPE and online.rainn.org) in partnership with more than 1,100 local rape crisis centers across the country, and operates the Safe Helpline (www.safehelpline.org/) for the Department of Defense. RAINN also carries out programs to prevent sexual violence, help victims, and ensure that sex offenders are brought to justice.

Security on Campus, Inc. (SOC)

www.securityoncampus.org/

SOC is dedicated to the prevention of criminal violence at colleges and universities nationwide through educational, awareness, and policy initiatives. It was cofounded in 1987 by Connie and Howard Clery following the rape and murder of their daughter at Lehigh University. In its efforts to advocate for more stringent campus security measures, SOC was a driving force behind the Clery Act and several subsequent amendments to this law. In addition to its public policy work, SOC provides Clery Act training, peer education, and victim advocacy and referral services.

United Educators (UE)

www.ue.org/home.aspx

UE, a reciprocal risk retention group, was created by educational institutions for educational institutions to provide a high-quality, specialized alternative to commercial insurance. UE offers a number of resources on campus sexual misconduct to its members.

Violence Against Women Online Resources (VAWOR)

www.vaw.umn.edu/

VAWOR is a collaborative project between the Minnesota Center Against Violence and Abuse (www.mincava.umn.edu/) and OVW. It provides resources to the general public, researchers, criminal justice practitioners, advocates, and social service professionals on research and promising practices on violence against women issues. The materials on the VAWOR Web site were developed by organizations with expertise in violence against women who provide technical assistance for grantees funded through OVW.

Publications

Archambault, Joanne. 2005. *Investigating Sexual Assaults Model Policy*. Alexandria, VA: International Association of Chiefs of Police, Inc., www.theiacp.org/tabid/299/Default.aspx?id=1133&v=1

Archambault, Joanne. 2005. *Investigating Sexual Assaults Part 1: Elements of Sexual Assault & Initial Response*. Alexandria, VA: International Association of Chiefs of Police, Inc., www.theiacp.org/tabid/299/Default.aspx?id=1144&v=1

Archambault, Joanne. 2005. *Investigating Sexual Assaults Part 2: Investigative Procedures*. Alexandria, VA: International Association of Chiefs of Police, Inc., www.theiacp.org/tabid/299/Default.aspx?id=1145&v=1

Archambault, Joanne. 2005. *Investigating Sexual Assaults Part 3: Investigative Strategy and Prosecution*. Alexandria, VA: International Association of Chiefs of Police, Inc., www.theiacp.org/tabid/299/Default.aspx?id=1146&v=1

Dedel, Kelly. 2011. *Sexual Assault of Women by Strangers*. Washington, DC: U.S. Department of Justice, Office of Community Oriented Policing Services, www.cops.usdoj.gov/files/RIC/Publications/e081115390_POPSexualAssault-508.pdf.

Eisenga, Harold. 2005. *Pre-Text Phone Calls in Sexual Assault Investigations*. Alexandria, VA: International Association of Chiefs of Police, Inc., www.theiacp.org/PublicationsGuides/TopicalIndex/tabid/216/Default.aspx?id=1147&v=1

Fisher, Bonnie S., Francis Cullen, and Michael Turner. 2000. *The Sexual Victimization of College Women*. Washington, DC: U.S. Department of Justice, www.nij.gov/pubs-sum/182369.htm.

Fisher, Bonnie S., et al. 2003. "Reporting Sexual Victimization to the Police and Others: Results From a National-Level Study of College Women." *Criminal Justice and Behavior*, 30(1), 6–38. Washington, DC: U.S. Department of Justice, http://cjb.sagepub.com/content/30/1/6.

Karjane, Heather M., Bonnie Fisher, and Francis Cullen. 2002. *Campus Sexual Assault: How America's Institutions of Higher Education Respond*. Washington, DC: U.S. Department of Justice, www.ncjrs.gov/pdffiles1/nij/grants/196676.pdf.

Karjane, Heather M., Bonnie Fisher, and Francis Cullen. 2005. *Sexual Assault on Campus: What Colleges and Universities Are Doing About It*. Washington, DC: U.S. Department of Justice, www.ncjrs.gov/pdffiles1/nij/205521.pdf.

Krebs, Christopher P., et al. 2007. *The Campus Sexual Assault Study Final Report*. Washington, DC: U.S. Department of Justice, www.ncjrs.gov/pdffiles1/nij/grants/221153.pdf.

Krebs, Christopher P., Kelle Barrick, and Christine Lindquist. 2011. *The Historically Black College and University Campus Sexual Assault Study*. Washington, DC: U.S. Department of Justice, www.ncjrs.gov/pdffiles1/nij/grants/233614.pdf.

Lawyer, Stephen, et al. 2010. "Forcible, Drug-Facilitated, and Incapacitated Rape and Sexual Assault Among Undergraduate Women." *Journal of American College Health*, 58(5), 453–460. See www.ncbi.nlm.nih.gov/pubmed/20304757 for the abstract.

Lisak, D., et al. 2010. "False Allegations of Sexual Assault: An Analysis of Ten Years of Reported Cases." *Violence Against Women*, 16(12), 1314–1334. See www.ncbi.nlm.nih.gov/pubmed/21164210 for the abstract.

Norris, J. 2008. *The Relationship Between Alcohol Consumption and Sexual Violence*. Harrisburg, PA: The National Resource Center on Domestic Violence, www.vawnet.org/Assoc_Files_VAWnet/AR_AlcVictimization.pdf.

Office for Civil Rights. 2011. *Sexual Violence Dear Colleague Letter Fact Sheet*. Washington, DC: U.S. Department of Education, www.ed.gov/ocr/docs/dcl-factsheet-201104.pdf.

Office for Civil Rights. 2011. *Sexual Violence Know Your Rights Document*. Washington, DC: U.S. Department of Education, www.ed.gov/ocr/docs/title-ix-rights-201104.pdf.

Office of Community Oriented Policing Services. 2007. *Campus Safety CD–ROM*. Washington, DC: U.S. Department of Justice, www.cops.usdoj.gov/RIC/ResourceDetail.aspx?RID=385.

Office of Community Oriented Policing Services. 2005. *National Summit on Campus Public Safety: Strategies for Colleges and Universities in a Homeland Security Environment.* Washington, DC: U.S. Department of Justice, www.cops.usdoj.gov/files/RIC/Publications/NationalSummitonCampusPublicSafety.pdf.

Sampson, Rana. 2011. *Acquaintance Rape of College Students*. Washington, DC: Office of Community Oriented Policing Services, www.cops.usdoj.gov/files/RIC/Publications/POPAcquaintanceRape-508.pdf.

Other Resources

State "Blue Prints"

Some states have developed plans and recommendations to strengthen their colleges' and universities' responses to sexual assault. For example—

- California Campus Sexual Assault Task Force's *California Campus Blueprint to Address Sexual Assault: Report to Governor Schwarzenegger and the California Legislature*, http://new.vawnet.org/Assoc_Files_VAWnet/CampusBlueprint.pdf; and *California State University Northridge Campus Plan to Address Sexual Assault*, http://www-admn.csun.edu/police/CSUN%20Sexual%20Assault%20Plan.pdf.

- Oregon's Attorney General's Sexual Assault Task Force offers a series of position papers, several of which are focused on campus issues: *Recommended Guidelines for Comprehensive Sexual Assault Response and Prevention on Campus*; *A Best Practice: Prioritizing a Victim-Centered Sexual Assault Response within Campus Alcohol Policies*; and *Recommended Policy for Higher Education Institutions: Guidelines for First Disclosure Recipients*. See http://oregonsatf.org/resources/satf-position-papers/ and www.oregonsatf.org/resources/docs/Campus_SA_Guidelines_Final.pdf.

Appendix: Summary of Applicable Federal Regulations

In cases involving sexual violence, schools must comply with state and federal laws that address sexual harassment, criminal offenses, sex offender registration, and child protection (mandatory reporting requirements), as well as several federal statutes and regulations related to crime on campus and privacy issues. Failure to comply with Title IX can potentially result in termination of federal funding or civil action against these institutions. In addition, under the Clery Act, the U.S. Department of Education can issue civil fines to postsecondary institutions that participate in the Higher Education Act's (HEA) Title IV student financial assistance programs of up to $27,500 per violation for a substantial misrepresentation of the number, location, or nature of the crimes required to be reported or for a violation of any other provision of the safety- and security-related HEA regulations. This section briefly reviews the federal statutes and regulations, including federal anti-discrimination laws.

Title IX of the Education Amendments of 1972

Title IX of the Education Amendments of 1972 (Title IX), 20 U.S.C. Sec. 1681, *et seq.*, prohibits discrimination on the basis of sex in education programs or activities operated by recipients of federal financial assistance. An April 4, 2011, Dear Colleague Letter issued by the U.S. Department of Education, Office for Civil Rights (OCR), reiterated that the requirements of Title IX cover sexual violence (physical sexual acts perpetrated against a person's will or where a person is incapable of giving consent) and reminded schools of their responsibilities to take immediate and effective steps to respond to sexual violence in accordance with Title IX. The Dear Colleague Letter (available at www.ed.gov/ocr/letters/colleague-201104.pdf)—

- Provides guidance on the concerns that arise in sexual violence cases, such as the role of criminal investigations and a school's independent responsibility under Title IX to investigate and address sexual violence.

- Provides guidance and examples about key Title IX requirements and how they relate to sexual violence.

- Discusses proactive efforts that schools can take to prevent sexual violence.

- Discusses the interplay between Title IX, the Family Educational Rights and Privacy Act, and the Clery Act, as it relates to a complainant's right to know the outcome of the complaint.
- Provides examples of remedies and enforcement strategies that schools and OCR may use to respond to sexual violence.

The Dear Colleague Letter summarizes the obligations of institutions of higher education under Title IX regarding sexual violence. Specifically, a school must—

- Take immediate and appropriate action to investigate or otherwise determine what occurred if it knows or reasonably should know of possible student-on-student sexual violence. The school's inquiry must be prompt, thorough, and impartial. If sexual violence has occurred, a school must take timely and effective steps to end the sexual violence, prevent its recurrence, and address its effects, regardless of whether it is the subject of a criminal investigation.
- Take steps to protect the complainant, as necessary, including interim steps taken prior to the final outcome of the investigation.
- Provide a grievance procedure for students to file complaints of sex discrimination, including complaints of sexual violence. These procedures must include an equal opportunity for both parties to present witnesses and other evidence, similar and timely access to any information that will be used at the proceeding, an equal opportunity for legal representation, and the same appeal rights.
- Use the preponderance-of-evidence standard to resolve complaints of sex discrimination in its grievance procedures.
- Notify in writing both parties of the outcome of the complaint.
- Ensure that its employees are trained so that they know to report harassment to appropriate school officials, and so that employees with the authority to address harassment know how to respond properly. Employees designated to serve as Title IX coordinators must have adequate training on what constitutes sexual harassment, including sexual violence, and how the school's grievance procedures operate. In addition, all campus public safety agency employees should receive training on the school's Title IX grievance procedures and any other procedures used for investigating reports of sexual violence.

The Clery Act

In 1990, Congress enacted the Crime Awareness and Campus Security Act of 1990 (Title II of Public Law 101-542), which amended the Higher Education Act of 1965 (HEA). This Act required all postsecondary institutions participating in HEA's Title IV student financial assistance programs to disclose campus crime statistics and security information. The Act was amended in 1992, 1998, and 2000. The 1998 amendments renamed the law the Jeanne Clery Disclosure of Campus Security Policy and Campus Crime Statistics Act in memory of a student who was slain in her dorm room in 1986. It is referred to as the Clery Act (Westat, 2011).

The Clery Act includes the following components:

- Institutions must publish an annual report disclosing campus security policies and 3 years' worth of selected crime statistics.
- Institutions must make timely warnings to the campus community about crimes that pose an ongoing threat to students and employees.
- Each institution with a police or security department must have a public crime log.
- The U.S. Department of Education must centrally collect and disseminate the crime statistics.
- Campus community sexual assault victims are assured of certain basic rights (see below).
- Both the accused and the accuser must be notified of the outcome[i] of any disciplinary proceeding involving a sex offense at the postsecondary level (Dear Colleague Letter, 14).
- Institutions that fail to comply may be fined or lose eligibility to participate in federal student aid programs.

The Handbook for Campus Safety and Security Reporting, available at www.ed.gov/admins/lead/safety/campus.html, includes additional information regarding each component.

The U.S. Congress enacted the Campus Sexual Assault Victims' Bill of Rights in 1992 as a part of the Higher Education Amendments of 1992 (PL 102-325, section 486(c)). It requires that all colleges and universities participating in federal student aid programs afford sexual assault victims certain basic rights. It also requires that schools notify victims of their option to report their assault to the proper law enforcement authorities. This bill of rights now is part of the campus security reporting requirements of the Clery Act. These rights include the following:

- The accuser and accused must have the same opportunity to have others present.
- Both parties shall be informed of the outcome of any disciplinary proceeding.
- Survivors shall be informed of their option to notify law enforcement.
- Survivors shall be notified of counseling services.
- Survivors shall be notified of options for changing academic and living situations.

Title IV of the Civil Rights Act of 1964

Title IV of the Civil Rights Act of 1964 (Title IV), 42 U.S.C. § 2000c, prohibits public school districts and colleges from discriminating against students on the basis of sex, among other bases. The U.S. Department of Justice enforces Title IV to ensure that all persons, regardless of their sex, are provided equal educational opportunities. More information regarding Title IV and sex-based discrimination and harassment can be found at www.justice.gov/crt/about/edu/types.php.

Family Educational Rights and Privacy Act

The Family Educational Rights and Privacy Act (FERPA), 20 USC 1232g; 34 C.F.R. Part 99, is a federal law that protects the privacy of student education records. The law applies to all schools that receive funds under an applicable program of the U.S. Department of Education.

- FERPA does not preclude a postsecondary institution's compliance with the timely warning provision of the Clery Act. FERPA recognizes that information can, in case of an emergency, be released without consent when needed to protect the health and safety of others.
- Campus law enforcement records are not education records protected by FERPA.
- In a confidential Title IX investigation, the alleged perpetrator may have a right to receive information about allegations kept as part of an "education record" (Dear Colleague Letter, 5).

- Postsecondary institutions may not require a complainant to abide by a nondisclosure agreement to obtain information that must be disclosed under the Clery Act (Dear Colleague Letter, 14).

- When conduct involves a crime of violence or a non-forcible sex offense, FERPA allows postsecondary institutions to disclose the "final results" of disciplinary proceedings to the complainant (even if the institution concluded that a violation was not committed) (Dear Colleague Letter, 13–14).

- Schools may disclose sanctions to the complainant where the sanction directly relates to the complainant at the elementary, secondary, and postsecondary levels (Dear Colleague Letter, 13).

- Postsecondary institutions may disclose "final results" of a disciplinary proceeding to anyone if it determines that the student is a perpetrator of a crime of violence or a nonforcible sex offense, and the student has committed a violation of the institution's rules and policies (Dear Colleague Letter, 14).

Also see www.ed.gov/policy/gen/guid/fpco/ferpa/index.html.

For guidance on the relationship between the Health Insurance Portability and Accountability Act and FERPA with respect to student health records, see www.ed.gov/policy/gen/guid/fpco/doc/ferpa-hipaa-guidance.pdf.

Appendix Endnotes

[i] Under the Clery Act, "outcome" means the institution's final determination with respect to the alleged sex offense and any sanctions imposed on the accused. 34 C.F.R. § 668.46(b)(11)(vi)(B).

Appendix References

Office for Civil Rights. 2011. *Sexual Violence Dear Colleague Letter Fact Sheet*. Washington, DC: U.S. Department of Education, www.ed.gov/ocr/docs/dcl-factsheet-201104.pdf.

Office for Civil Rights. 2011. *Sexual Violence Know Your Rights Document*. Washington, DC: U.S. Department of Education, www.ed.gov/ocr/docs/title-ix-rights-201104.pdf.

Westat. 2011. *The Handbook for Campus Safety and Security Reporting.* Washington, DC: U.S. Department of Education, Office of Postsecondary Education, http://www2.ed.gov/admins/lead/safety/handbook.pdf

Acknowledgments

This report reflects the opinions, experiences, and expertise of the participants of the *Campus Sex Crimes Forum*. OVC is grateful for their input and recommendations. Participants included the following:

David Adams, Senior Policy Advisor, U.S. Department of Justice, Office of Justice Programs, Bureau of Justice Assistance

Jeff Allison, Special Advisor for Campus Public Safety, U.S. Department of Justice, Federal Bureau of Investigation

Nazmia Alqadi, Program Analyst, U.S. Department of Justice, Community Oriented Policing Services*

Michael Alsup, Police Chief, Harper College

Ted Baran, Director of Public Safety, Gallaudet University

Peter Berry, Chief Staff Officer, International Association of Campus Law Enforcement Administrators

Myrta Charles, Program Manager, U.S. Department of Justice, Office on Violence Against Women*

John Firman, Research Center Director, International Association of Chiefs of Police

Joye Frost, Acting Director, U.S. Department of Justice, Office of Justice Programs, Office for Victims of Crime*

Anne Glavin, Chief of Police/Director of Police Services, California State University–Northridge

Bea Hanson, Principal Deputy Director, U.S. Department of Justice, Office on Violence Against Women

Steven Healy, Managing Partner, Margolis, Healy & Associates

Calvin Hodnett, Management Analyst, U.S. Department of Justice, Community Oriented Policing Services

Leroy James, Chief of Police, Howard University

Phillip Johnson, Immediate Past President, International Association of Campus Law Enforcement Administrators*

Robb Jones, Vice President and General Counsel, United Educators

Diane Kelley, Naval Criminal Investigative Service Senior Representative to U.S. Department of Defense, Office of Inspector General, Investigative Policy and Oversight

Connie Kirkland, Director, Sexual Assault Services, George Mason University

Alison Kiss, Executive Director, Security on Campus, Inc.

Aviva Kurash, Senior Project Manager, International Association of Chiefs of Police

Mike Lynch, Chief of Police, George Mason University Police Department

Ada Meloy, General Counsel, American Council on Education

Jacqueline Michaels, Supervisory Attorney, U.S. Department of Education, Office for Civil Rights

Adrienne Meador Murray, Chief of Police, Davidson College

Cynthia Pappas, Senior Social Science Analyst, U.S. Department of Justice, Community Oriented Policing Services

Karen L. Pennington, Vice President, Montclair State University

Michael Rizzo, Project Manager, International Association of Chiefs of Police

Lynn Rosenthal, White House Advisor on Violence Against Women, Office of the Vice President

Marnie Shiels, Attorney Advisor, U.S. Department of Justice, Office on Violence Against Women (on detail to the Office for Victims of Crime)

Gina Maisto Smith, Partner, Ballard Spahr

Paul Verrecchia, President, International Association of Campus Law Enforcement Administrators*

Joseph Vess, Director of Training and Technical Assistance, Men Can Stop Rape

Rachel Weinstein, Staff Attorney, U.S. Department of Education, Office for Civil Rights*

*Indicates a participant also was a forum planning committee member.

OVC also thanks the following individuals for their involvement in planning the forum:

Jasmine D'Addario-Fobian, Victim Justice Program Specialist, National Training and Program Development Division, Office for Victims of Crime

Carroll Ann Ellis, Training Delivery Program Manager, Office for Victims of Crime Training and Technical Assistance Center

Aisha Johnson, Logistics Manager, Office for Victims of Crime Training and Technical Assistance Center

Lisa Phillips, Director of Government Relations, International Association of Campus Law Enforcement Administrators

Julie Stricker, Anti-Human Trafficking Training Specialist, Office for Victims of Crime Training and Technical Assistance Center

Appreciation goes to Kristin Littel for assisting with planning and facilitating the forum and authoring this report.